Today, in Therapy.

S.T. Venema

I0192161

Today, in Therapy
S.T. Venema

For Cabe, who was the encouragement I needed the most in the darkest times.

Hey there, how've you been? It's good to finally see you here. To tell you the truth there have been more than a few times over the years of writing this that this book almost didn't happen. This is actually my sixth time writing this thing and I think it's high time that I share it with you.

Over the years I kept changing things, moving things around, adding and removing things, and all together scrapping it a few times. Some versions have focused on specific themes or tones, but I never quite liked any of them. For a while I had considered giving up on the project and just keeping the writing to myself, that is, until July of 2023.

In July of 2023 I hit a pretty low spot and finally started seeing a counselor. This was much by the encouragement of a few people close to me, including one good friend and coworker. I had shown him some of my writing which I had always used as an outlet when things got rough, and he encouraged me to keep writing and to share that writing with other people. He always told me that the art we create out of pain is some of the purest representations of ourselves, and that maybe we can use that art to encourage others who are going through the same problems in life. It is a way to show people that they are never alone in their struggles.

While I was writing this I kept falling back on the same issue that I had faced the first five times. I had no idea how to organize this book in a way that conveyed what I wanted it to. It was in one of my counseling sessions that I figured it out. My counselor had made a comment that the process of healing is never cut and dried. There are always ups and downs and sometimes things get worse again in the middle of them getting better. There are no clear benchmarks that you'll know you've hit as soon as you hit them, you only see it after the fact. That is how I wanted to structure this book. There are no clear chapters or sections, there are no dividing points between darker and lighter tones, there is only a gradual shift in mood.

In July of 2023, while I was working at a liquor store, I spent a lot of slow nights sitting on a stack of milk crates with a pen and a pad of paper. A lot of nights were spent having good conversations with that friend about everything going on in life at the time. On one of those nights I wrote a poem and the first three words just stuck in my mind. Those three words have gotten me to where I am right now, sharing my story with you so that hopefully, whatever you are going through, you can see that your burdens have been carried before.

Today, in therapy...

I would like to offer a trigger warning before you dive in. Some of the topics discussed are sensitive for many people. I have attempted to give the truest image of myself in this book and that image is often not the most uplifting.

TODAY, IN THERAPY

If I could take a photograph of depression
It would be of a smiling, happy person
Who shows no hint of sadness except in the corner of their eye.
Depression is rarely seen on the outside.
It's bottled up, tucked away,
Out of the frame.
It's in the sink where the dishes have piled up because loading the
dishwasher is too big of a burden.
It's in the ever growing list of phone calls that need to be made but
haven't been because there is no energy to speak.
It's in the plans with friends that keep being canceled
And in all the dirty floors.
Depression is never as easy as being in the frame of a photograph.
So if I could take a photograph of depression
You'd never know it was there at all.

It's been a few months now since I've polished my boots.
I haven't shaved in three weeks
And I'm overdue for a haircut.
The dishes have piled up in the kitchen sink.
My laundry has gathered in a pile on the bathroom floor.
The kitchen needs sweeping and the living room needs to be vacuumed.
My curtains haven't let light into my house for a week.
It would all take twenty minutes to fix
But every step, every breath,
They drain me.
I just don't have the energy today
And that's okay.
There's always tomorrow.

TODAY, IN THERAPY

It seems that my life always boils down to this
Awake
Alone
In my car in a parking lot with my thoughts
Wondering where I went wrong this time
I lost track a long time ago of the miles I've driven to answer that
question

I think I'm going insane.
Slowly, but not as slowly as I'd like to.
There's a heart beating under my floorboards.
There's a black cat cemented into the wall of my cellar.
I think I'm going insane.
When Cthulhu put madness into the minds of men he was fulfilling a vendetta against me.
I want to get out of here.
I NEED to get out of here.
Out of this job,
Out of this house,
Out of this town,
Out of my mind.
Let me out.
Let me out!
LET ME OUT!

TODAY, IN THERAPY

I haven't been happy in quite some time.
It's nobody's fault
Except, perhaps, my own.

They say money can't buy happiness
But that isn't because it's not for sale.
I just don't have the money
And the prices have gone to hell.

TODAY, IN THERAPY

I once had a bamboo.
It grew in the corner of my living room.
A small apartment
And a dream.

Oh how hopeful I was!
And foolish.
You see,
The nasty business about hope
And having it
Is that the world will,
Soon enough,
Rob you of it.

It may be a thing with feathers
But rent, bills, a job, depression,
Those things are the shotgun.
And landlords, bosses, family,
The finger on the trigger.

I once had a bamboo
When I could afford my small apartment
And my dreams.

I think I'm going a little bit crazy
But maybe I've always been a bit insane.
I mean, I don't know what it is that I'm doing
Or even what it is that I'm supposed to be doing.
I've lived the life of someone twice my age.
I bounce around a lot,
I travel,
I experience as much as I can while I can.
The world is my stage.
I guess part of it is that I can't sit still
And part of it is that I never expected myself to live this long in the
first place.
As is,
I feel like I'm pushing my luck.
I can feel the decay.
Maybe I do it all because deep down I know that the day I can't be
this free is the day life ends anyways,
And I think that I know what I'd do to myself after that.
None of it really matters but I guess it should matter to me while
I'm here.
Maybe I'm a nihilist of sorts,
I don't know.
I just think that there's something deeply wrong with me.
I guess I've always had the suspicion.
My mind likes to play tricks on itself while my body hits the self
destruct button.
I don't have a very strong sense of self preservation.
Adrenaline is my drug of choice
And maybe I should get some help
But antidepressants are hell

TODAY, IN THERAPY

And I'd sooner throw myself off of a mountain with a finicky parachute for a chance to feel alive.

I don't mind the counseling sessions though because it's nice to be heard even if I'm still not really understood.

Maybe it's just the society I'm stuck in.

Maybe it's the focus on work, eat, sleep, repeat that I can't stand.

Maybe I'll quit my job.

Maybe I'll move to Bozeman.

Maybe I'll open a bookstore in a coastal town in Maine.

Maybe I'll keep going insane.

Maybe I'll die when I'm 25.

Maybe I still won't know what I'm doing.

Anyways,

Other than that I'm okay.

It's good running into you like this.

How about you? How've you been?

Something in my bones feels broken today.
Except it isn't my bones,
It's in my soul.
It's in my will to carry on.
It's in the stuff that holds my shape.
Internal,
Unseen,
Broken.

TODAY, IN THERAPY

I pick up that old razor
And return the tired old gaze
To the man looking back at me
From behind the mirror.

I think to myself
"Chuck B,
You son of a bitch.
You're right again."

For the ferns are dead
And my potted plants are as yellow as corn
Dried up in the fields.

You were right about pain,
And its absurdities.
About existing and nothing more.

And Charles,
In a sense you were right about the world
Because it has failed the both of us.

Heaven is but a place
Where the fools fall in love.
And Hell,
A home for the lonely hearts
And broken souls.

TODAY, IN THERAPY

The abyss calls me.
"Jump," she says,
"Down into my depths."
Oh how sweetly she sings.
"Come into my eternity.
Be at peace with me."
The tempting whispers
Of final rest.

The personification of my dreams
Dismembered in front of my eyes.
My God! My God,
The screams,
As the reaper sings
Sweet doubts into my ear,
So gentle.
And while I may be alive in my body
It is not the same inside of my head.
For a life like this,
Void of living,
Means I might as well be dead.

TODAY, IN THERAPY

My life has become a casual suicide.
Stepping into the street without looking for traffic.
Driving in the dark without my headlights.
I ignore the dull aches and pains in hope that my ailments may become critical.
I tend to stand a little too close to the edges of high places.
My seatbelt is a cage which traps me in my misery.
I often neglect my coat in the snow.
My life has become a downword spiral.
Self neglect,
Self hate,
Self harm.
And I often hope that someday some fate befalls me.
Oh how lucky I will be when my luck runs dry.

Life has been kicking my ass lately.
My weeks all blow up in my face,
My engine blew up in my face,
My tires blew up in my face,
And my debt blew up in my face.
I can't catch a break.
Sometimes the only option we have is to pull ourselves up,
Wash off the blood and dust,
And choose to win.

TODAY, IN THERAPY

The clouds are even darker today.
Heavier. Burdened, and closer to the earth.
It makes the air feel thicker.
It's going to take a double dose of sunshine to keep me on my feet
today;
To keep me from stumbling down the jagged rocky path.

But the pill bottle is empty now.
There will be no second dose, no,
Not even a first.
And so, I blow the clouds away,
Taking aim at the sky with the barrel beneath my chin.

The clouds and I fade away,
As if having never existed at all.

The flies keep buzzing around me
And the vultures watch me from the trees.
Even they know how dead and cold I feel.

TODAY, IN THERAPY

A razor blade on the bathroom vanity,
The sharpest one he could find.
He did it again, isn't that insanity?
He must be losing his mind.
But he fell for the lies and the look in her eyes
When she told him that she would stay true.
So he said his goodbyes and he muffled his cries,
Put the blade to his wrist and cut through.

S.T. VENEMA

Above all else
Being ignored
Makes me feel more alone
Than having nobody around at all.

TODAY, IN THERAPY

We've all felt it at least once.
Your heart drops to the pit of your stomach,
Grinding your hopes into shit.
It came for me last December.
A late night argument.
A suicide note left in my small, dark apartment.
She was gone.
My heart dropped into my gut
As my soul left me through a deep sigh.
Realization hits us like a truck sometimes.
I know what it's like,
Coming home to nothing
Except a note on yellow paper.

Yet here I am, myself,
Writing my letter.

Slice.
Another mark.
A few red beads of blood.
Soon to be another scar.
Such as it often was when I was young.
Slice.
Another one to cover
Under denim jeans,
Where nobody will see it.
Slice.
Just searching for feeling.
Pain, regret, anything.
Anything but numb.
Slice.
Tomorrow it will repeat.
Put the mask on
And pretend to be okay.
Slice.
Another day,
Another eternity.
I could end it now.
Just cut a little deeper.
Slice.

TODAY, IN THERAPY

"Any thoughts of self harm, suicide, or hurting anyone else?"
No.
I don't think I've ever really answered that question honestly.
Because, to me,
The only thing worse than fighting my wars,
Is allowing other people to dictate the rules of battle.

The things that nobody sees
About me and my history.
What they don't know
About my trials
And my battles.
The things they never know
About the stress and anxiety
That keeps me up at night.
About the self-loathing
And the hatred for the man in the mirror.
The things nobody sees.
All of the loneliness
And the pain.
About the heartbreak and the heartache.
The backstabbing and the betrayal.
The things they don't feel.
The anger, and the rage
That burns inside me endlessly.
No ocean can quench that fire.
The things nobody knows.
The thoughts that render me sleepless.
The stygian depths of my mind.
Relentless demons and self-sabotage.
The things I tried to hide.
The day it became too heavy to carry on
And my burdens almost crushed me.

TODAY, IN THERAPY

I think that
Far too many of us
Are only really wanted
For as long as we are useful.

"Men don't cry"
Except for the men who comprise 60% of homeless people in America.
Men don't cry
Except for the ones who compile 95% of combat deaths.
Men don't cry
Except for those in 60% of workplace injuries
And 90% of workplace deaths.
Men don't cry
Except for the 105 who take their own lives every day in the United States,
Totaling 79% of U.S. suicides.
Men don't cry
Except for the ones who feel nothing but pressure to be providers
And feel like they've failed when they can no longer provide.
Except for the ones whose only value according to society is measured by what they can produce.
Men don't cry
Except for the fathers who are inherently less likely to win custody battles and only get to see their children on the weekends.
Men don't cry
Because society refuses to give a damn about them
And spits them out when they cease to be of use.
Men don't cry?
Or do you just choose not to see it
Because it only happens behind closed doors
In solitude?
"Men don't cry"
That's bull shit.

TODAY, IN THERAPY

As a man, I weep for the men who have been trampled over.
I weep for the men who society left behind.
As a man,
I cry.
And as a man, you have my permission to cry too.
You are not weak.
You are not a failure.
You have value.
So cry
And I will be here to cry with you.

The air here is dirty.
Thick, heavy, black.
Filthy.
I try to get outside to see the sun once in a while
But there is no sun,
And no sky,
And no air.
The sky carries a weight here.
The weight of industry,
Of "progress."
But the air doesn't carry bird songs
Or ocean spray
Or the sweet smell of the forest in may.
The air here chokes me;
Beats me into submission,
Until I, too, become just another brick in the wall.
I too become another cog in the machine, pumping smoke into the
already smoke choked air.
Into my smoke choked lungs.
Killing the birds.
Silencing their songs.

TODAY, IN THERAPY

It was a good day today on the surface.
Work went well.
I stayed busy.
But I don't have much interest in things today.
I'm overthinking again.
I've been tired all day but now it's midnight and I still can't sleep.
I can't stand it,
Always feeling numb.
Depression is not just unhappiness,
It's the force that sucks out the ability to feel happy
Even when good things happen.
Therapy starts Monday I guess.
I just want to feel okay again.
Anyways,
Goodnight.

The leaves.
The temperatures.
The snow.
My mood.
My standards.
My hope.

Some of the things dropping to the ground this time of year.

TODAY, IN THERAPY

I don't really want to be alive anymore.
Not right now at least.
I don't want to be alive, not in the way that I wish to die,
I've grown past that,
But in the way that I don't want to live in this time and space
And these circumstances.
I want to be alive in the way that I was last summer,
Singing and dancing and living underneath endless western skies.
I want to be alive in the way that I will be next month
When life returns to normal.
Living life with all of my missing pieces.
I even want to be be alive in the way that I picture myself being alive
a year from now,
Away from this town, these people,
These circumstances.
Happier, at least as I imagine it now.
But right now, as it stands, I don't really want to be alive anymore.
Not in the manner that I want to kill myself,
But rather, in the manner in which I want to kill this part of myself.
I don't want to be alive right now, not really.
But more than I want to not be alive I want to be free to live.
Free of these places and these people,
Free of these burdens and stresses,
And free of these circumstances.
Free to exist in a space
Where I no longer feel like I no longer want to be alive.

It was June and I was 22,
Sitting in the waiting room of a hospital,
As I so often find myself.
Folded up and tucked away safely
In my back right pocket, behind my wallet,
Was a hastily written letter.
It contained a short list of names and phone numbers;
People I could trust for small favors
And those who I was obligated to keep informed about any developments in my condition.
On the back of the letter was a crudely formulated will,
Just a handful of last requests should the worst happen.
I want to be cremated, then toss my ashes into the sea.
The Islands were my home once and that's where I want to be.

No funerals! They're insufferable and lame.
Use the money for a vacation then have a cookout in my name.
Give my brother my rifle, my vest, and battle belt
In the event that I succumb to the hand that I've been dealt.
Now this one is important and it's for the people I love.
Just know I'm always with you, looking down from Heaven above.
I always wanted to travel, so everywhere you roam
Know that I'm traveling also, up in my heavenly home.
Now go and see the world, and know that I love you.
I'll see you soon in Heaven when your well lived days are through.

It was June and I was 22
And I was sitting in the waiting room of a hospital,
As I so often find myself doing.

TODAY, IN THERAPY

I took my note, unfolded it, and read it for the seventh time that morning
As if it had somehow rewritten itself.
When I had once again numbed myself to my own words I folded and returned the note to my pocket
While trying, myself, not to fold.
My girlfriend's mother had come with me and she gave me a reassuring look,
A difficult feat for her.
The doctor should be coming through those giant wooden doors any moment now;
Those gates to both Heaven and Hell.
I wasn't entirely sure if I should feel scared or sad or even angry.
Nobody really tells you those things
And you're not really prepared to die
When it's June and you're 22.

My legs carry my body shakily across the floor.
From room to room,
Down bland beige hallways,
And past identical cubicles.
It's as if my legs take me against the will of my heart.
My eyes look around me.
Sad white and blue spheres.
A hopeless gaze.
My hands are heavy,
As if being chained to my desk.
I move from one task to the next.
From one eternity to the next.
Anything to get to five,
And five of those days to Friday.
A five second weekend.
Repeat.

TODAY, IN THERAPY

There's a photograph of me in an album on my bookshelf.
The face is younger, the hair is fuller, the smile is more genuine.
But the eyes seem to grow old with me.
The eyes look older and duller and deeper and more hurt with each passing day,
Like some version of Dorian Gray.
My own eyes are failing now
And a fog is creeping over the photograph.
What happened to the man smiling into the camera lens?

Monday, October 14, 2019.
The thing that I remember the most clearly
Is how nobody was there for me the night that I tried to kill myself.
The night that I needed them the most.
October 14, 2019.
All I needed was one person, I tried calling ten.
Ten unanswered calls and texts.
When I asked my friends to grab lunch
They were too tired.
When I tried to call my family
They were too busy.
I was the most alone I have ever been in my whole life.
I was alone
When I missed my 10:00 am class
Because every single time I tried to leave my bed the chains in my mind and the weight on my heart pulled me back into my mattress.
I was alone
When nobody even noticed that I was late to work
Because my shoes turned into cinder blocks when I laced them onto my feet.
I was alone
When I texted my friends
And I told them that I just needed someone to talk to for a while but the messages were left on open.
I was alone
When I walked from my college dorm room to the bluffs in the dead of night.
The clouds had blotted out the stars, keeping me continually in the dark.

TODAY, IN THERAPY

The wind had whipped up the lake and the water was as black as the night.
As turbulent as the thoughts which flooded my mind
And drowned out any reason
And any hope.
That void had been calling out my name for a very long time, the only one who ever called.
And this time I was going to answer it.
I was alone
When I stepped up to that ledge and screamed at God
Because it felt like even He wasn't listening to me when I was begging him for help.
How wrong I was.
A step forward.
Fifty feet down.
A fall that lasted an eternity.
The ice-cold water took every inch of air out of my lungs the second I pierced into the depths.
In all the chaos the seconds blurred into hours and for once the thoughts stopped swirling.
For the first time in years I felt calm.
At peace.
I was alone
When the world around me faded to black and I accepted that this was the end.
That I was meant to be the one people pretended to give a damn about when my name was mentioned.
The one people would say they wished they had seen the warning signs like I hadn't painted them on the wall myself.
Like my last text hadn't been left open.

But I guess God had other plans.

I was still alone

Six hours later when I washed up on a stone covered beach and realize that, like so many times before,

I had failed.

Superior never gives up her dead but even she had spat me back out.

Yes, I had failed to end my own existence,

But I had failed myself.

For several hours I laid on that beach, half way in the water hoping that the cold would finish the job.

I don't know when I stood up

Or what gave me the strength to get on my feet.

I don't remember how long it took me to walk back home in the early hours of October 15.

But the thing I remember the most clearly

Is that nobody was there for me when I got back

And not a single person ever did reply to me or check in to see what was going on.

I remember very clearly

That I was alone.

TODAY, IN THERAPY

My eyes are heavy today
Like big, glass marbles.
The sun is warm, if not a bit too sharp and bright to them.
The dark is far too cold and empty.
My eyes are heavy today,
But not in the sense of being tired.
They're just heavy from the weight of all they have seen,
Weighed down by countless burdens.

Days like this are the hardest for me.
So many stupid little things,
All piling up.
All the little inconveniences.
All the major problems.
There is, seemingly, no end in sight;
No benchmark for either success or failure.
So it all feels like failure.
These are the kinds of days that slowly break me.

TODAY, IN THERAPY

Hey, how's it going?
Good, and you?
Not too bad.

We are both fucking liars.

I don't really know when the switch happened, but I do know how my friends reacted.
It all started with the jokes about suicide,
And then passive comments made out of mild frustration.
But somewhere along the way the comments became more frequent
And the jokes became more serious.
My friends who had laughed and joked along were no longer laughing.
"Are you okay bro?"
I guess I wasn't,
But at the time I couldn't see it.
To me they were still just jokes and passing remarks.
You see,
The difference between thinking something and saying it is that the spoken word is as firm as concrete.
It holds weight over you.
Manifestation is power.

TODAY, IN THERAPY

It's been
One thing after another
For a year now,
Or maybe a bit more.
I forget.

I can't catch a break.

Some days I just don't have the energy
To pick myself up off the floor.
And some days I don't have the strength
To keep going like this anymore.
It's getting difficult again
To carry on the fight
So, I guess, until tomorrow
Goodnight.

TODAY, IN THERAPY

I found myself in a hospital waiting room today.
The emergency department.
I was there for something relatively minor,
Just one of those mishaps that life brings.
As I sat there, silently, to the side,
I realized once again how curious a place a hospital waiting room
can be.
A cut finger,
Pancreatitis,
A broken bone.
Just a few of the things I happened to overhear.
But as I sat there, waiting to be seen, something happened.
In came a man who broke my heart.
Even though we had never met, I knew him.
I knew him by the defeated look in his eyes, and by the tears
streming down his face.
He walked into the waiting room, shaking and sobbing.

He wiped the tears from his cheek
And in a voice too meek for a man so large
He asked the receptionist
"Is this where you go if you're suicidal?"

8 billion people in this world.
332 million in the U.S.
10 million just in Michigan.
There are 9,000 people in my town.

So why the hell do most of us feel so alone?

TODAY, IN THERAPY

Life.
It's a sexually transmitted
Chronic illness
With a 100% mortality rate.
Godspeed.
Have fun.

S.T. VENEMA

I saw that photo on the shelf
And knew that I had broken a promise to myself.
The cliff above the water,
The one that almost ended me,
And I realize that once again I had sunk that low.
But I'll get better, eventually, I know.

TODAY, IN THERAPY

It does feel good to be free for a while
Even though it feels like everything else around me
Is burning down
To ashes.

Sometimes I wonder about what happened in the other timelines.
The one where I missed the wave when I jumped
And broke myself open on the rocks
And never washed up on the beach.
How would life go on?
For my friends, my family, and for all of the people who I would
never meet?
I never would have traveled,
Seen the mountains
Or explored the islands in a kayak.
I never would have had all of those memories.
What about the timeline where I didn't hit the brakes
And let my car fly off the curve and wrap around a tree?
I never would have talked to my friends again.
They would think that they had failed me because they couldn't
make me hold on for just another day.
I would never have written this.
And had the honor and the privilege of you reading it.
I wouldn't have had the chance to give the hope that I so
desperately needed whenI was at my lowest.
Don't let the darkness fool you
The sun will shine again
Even if it takes a while to break through the clouds.
I still haven't healed yet
But I'm getting there.
I'm starting over.
Some days are still shit
But when i think of the other timelines,
The ones where I didn't have the strength to hold on,

TODAY, IN THERAPY

I thank God that this one is mine.

S.T. VENEMA

I once discussed with a friend
The dangers and the merits of romanticizing suicide
In art,
Specifically in music and poetry.
But here I am,
And some would say I'm doing just that.
Some would be fools for thinking so,
As foolish as I had once been.

TODAY, IN THERAPY

Two stacks of milk crates behind the old wooden counter.
Closing shift at the liquor store on a summer Saturday night.
Sometimes those talks were the most effective therapy.

It's alright if you lose your mind.
You can have a piece of mine
And some peace of mind.
Don't worry, take your time.
It's okay if you go insane
But don't forget your own name
And be sure not to stay there for too long.

TODAY, IN THERAPY

Sometimes the best way to be happy
Is to learn who to let go of.

I have always loved the ocean.
I find it mesmerizing.
The ebbs and flows,
The highs and lows,
The wave cycles.
I love the way that the waves rock my boat gently on calm days
And how I've fought to stay afloat in the largest gales.
My mind is like that ocean
But I always found it far less beautiful.
The highs are rare and the lows seem to last for eternities.
But still, when I compare the two of them
My mind is just as vast and deep;
Filled with wonderful and terrifying things.
All of it is worth exploring yet so little of it ever has been.
I've been stuck at a low tide for quite a while now
And I usually hate that.
I hate always feeling shallow, dry, numb.
But low tides show us the things we can't normally see
And while it shows the ugly, like a washed up bristle worm,
It 's where we see the most intricate and beautiful creatures,
Tucked away in the tide pools.
My mind is an ocean
And like the ocean I have to learn to appreciate all of it as a whole.
The highs and lows, the tide pools and the open seas,
The good and the bad.
And, like the ocean, my mind in its entirety
Is beautiful.

TODAY, IN THERAPY

"It's all in your head."
No shit.
That's the whole point,
I want to get it out of there.
It's all in my head.
Is that any excuse not to treat an aneurysm?
Or a brain tumor?

I'm not expecting you to be the strong one today.
You don't always have to provide,
Or carry the weight of the world.
Just for today
Kick off your boots
And hang up your hat.
You're no less of a man for it.

TODAY, IN THERAPY

It isn't always your fault.
Sometimes it just doesn't matter how hard you try.
You can do everything right
Completely flawlessly.
You can give it your all
And it still doesn't work.
It all still falls apart.
Sometimes we just fail
And that's okay.
Pick yourself up and keep trying.

It hasn't been good lately.
The clouds came back and the rain began to pour.
I know it's only temporary
But days like today make things better.
It's some sort of relief.

TODAY, IN THERAPY

I really do wish you the best.
Just understand that, sometimes,
The journey to what's best
Really fucking hurts.

Sometimes getting out of bed and taking a shower is enough.
If that's all you can do then you gave 100%.
Dishes and laundry can wait until tomorrow.

TODAY, IN THERAPY

God gave me another day.
What a wonderful gift!
How am I going to thank Him with it?

Things start to change when you get fed up with your own bull shit.
So,
Are you annoyed yet?

TODAY, IN THERAPY

Decisions are best made with level heads.
So please,
Don't let go.
Not yet.

I got a tap on my window last night
While sleeping in a nearly empty parking lot.
The cop shined a blindingly bright flash light in my eyes.
"Hey, doing alright?"
"Yeah, just catching a few hours of sleep. Drove from Michigan today."
"Okay bud, just saw you here and wanted to make sure you were alright."
Sometimes it's nice to know people care
Even if it is just a stranger doing their job.

TODAY, IN THERAPY

I think it's pretty safe to say that I'm a broken man.
It's not that much of a stretch.
But to admit that has always felt like failure to me before now.
I hide the broken pieces as best I can,
Sweeping them under the rug.
I don't think it's just me that feels this way.
I look around myself and see millions of men who are all struggling
to barely hold on.
Millions who all feel as though they have failed
Simply for not being perfect.
I see them killing themselves all the time,
Once literally.
Hell, even I tried once.
Half of the problem is that we just don't want to talk about it,
As if we don't face mental challenges too.
It's a stigma that I'm really fucking tired of.
So let me let you in on a secret,
Man to man.
You're not alone, as cheesy as it feels to say so.
Broken pieces can always be mended.
You haven't failed anyone, especially yourself.
Don't try to run from the challenges in your head.
Don't just hide the broken pieces.
Be a man and fight your battles.
From one broken man to another, I believe in you.
You'll beat this.
I'm proud of you.

People will let you down every single time.
Be content in your own company
And put your trust in God.
Just don't let other people steal your happiness
Or your hope.

TODAY, IN THERAPY

It took me four hours to leave bed today
And two to shower
But I made it to work today.
Progress is slow but it is progress nonetheless.

It's not over until I win.

TODAY, IN THERAPY

Do not become a secondary character in your own story.
Stay true to yourself above all else.
You are not just the sum of your circumstances
Or of those around you
Or even of everything that you've been through.
Be your own main character,
You badass.

S.T. VENEMA

I don't have to make it to next year.
I don't even need to make it to next month
Or next week
Or Tuesday.
I just need to give myself one more day.
Death can wait for me for two days.

TODAY, IN THERAPY

"That'll be $11.75."
He sounded tired.
A kind of tired that reaches deep into the soul.
I pulled around to the first window
With a credit card in my hand.
"How's it going tonight?" He asked.
The words were those of a zombie.
"I'm okay, how about you?"
"Not too bad."
But as I handed him my card I said something that surprised the both of us.
"You're lying."
He smiled faintly, took my card, and disappeared behind the sliding window.
A moment later he handed the card back.
"Hang in there man."
"Thanks." He said.
This time he was sincere.

Don't be angry at yourself for the things you did and said while you were just trying to survive.

While circumstances never excuse actionsas acceptable we all need a little forgiveness.

I forgive you.

TODAY, IN THERAPY

I can tell I'm starting to get better again.
Just a little bit, but it's an improvement.
I'm taking pride in my achievements again
Instead of just feeling relieved for having accomplished a task.
See, I have a hard time feeling happy even when good things happen,
But lately the good things make me feel a little less numb.
It's a slow start,
But a start nonetheless.

In case nobody has told you recently:
I'm proud of you,
Thank you for staying,
And you are so worthy and deserving of love
Because you are human and you are alive and that is a beautiful and
wonderful thing.
We all need to hear it sometimes and we so seldom do.
I know I need it.

TODAY, IN THERAPY

We live within the boundaries that we create for ourselves.

The longest nights create the most brilliant sunrises.
Violent storms make calm seas more peaceful.
The evergreens stand out best in the snow.
It's the toughest things in life that pay off
And it's the hardest battles that give the biggest victories.
It's the worst days that make us appreciate the best times.

TODAY, IN THERAPY

Today, in therapy, I was asked about my outlets and my coping mechanisms.

I told Derrick I do a lot of writing.

The deeper into the void I am pulled the purer the content I produce.

When ink on my skin can't make me feel any less numb I try to make ink on my paper do the trick.

Besides, tattoos are expensive and paper is cheap.

It doesn't always help

But I try it nonetheless

Because even if it can't make me feel anything, maybe someday it will help someone else.

Derrick told me to keep writing.

I've been told that before under different circumstances.

To tell you the truth I don't know if it's pulling me out of the hole or pushing me deeper.

Maybe it just passes the time,

The eternities that lay between the seconds when I feel better.

When I feel like myself.

I don't really know what "myself" feels like anymore.

It's been so long.

Maybe "myself" isn't meant to feel like anything other than exactly how I feel right now.

After all, past versions of me are dead, and the future me doesn't yet exist.

Maybe someday I'll figure out the big secret of how to be happy.

That ever elusive answer.

But until then I'll do what Derrick said, and keep writing

Because paper is cheaper than tattoos.

Dear younger me
Sit still for just a moment.
There are things I want to tell you.
There are things that you should hear.
There are things that you should know

Dear younger me
Don't be in such a hurry all the time.
I promise, things will work out just fine.
Slow down, enjoy the ride,
And don't hold yourself to other people's standards all the time.

Dear younger me
Don't give up on your dreams.
Remember what makes you happy
And never let go of those things.
Don't you ever stop roaming.
Don't live a life you find boring.

Dear younger me
Slow down a little bit.
Take care of yourself better.
Be gentle to your body
And be gentle to your mind.

Dear younger me
Sometimes, you really should know
When to keep holding on
And when to let it go.

TODAY, IN THERAPY

Some things should stay in the past.
Give yourself the room to grow.

Dear younger me
I know how scared you feel.
I know about the anxiety.
I know you feel like you are faking the confident face you put on,
But I see you now,
And that face is both deserved and real.

Dear younger me
Keep on working hard
And don't stop fighting for what you want,
But don't be afraid to ask for help.
You can lean on people once in a while.

Dear younger me
I know you haven't been happy for some time.
I know your burdens because they once were mine.

Dear younger me
I know you haven't had a reason why in a while
But trust me
Don't you ever lose your smile.

My best writing comes from the worst pain
So when the quality begins to fade
I know that it's been a good day.

TODAY, IN THERAPY

Go find yourself first,
And then
Never stop searching.

One good thing.
Just pick one good thing about today
And hold onto it.
It could be the smallest thing
Like having a green light at the intersection
Or finding a nickel on the floor.
Just find something good about today and hold on.
Don't let anyone take it from you.
Maybe even keep it a secret,
All for yourself.
That will get you through some dark days.

TODAY, IN THERAPY

The healing process is like jumping into a raging sea from a
helicopter,
Like a Coast Guard rescue swimmer.
The water comes at you fast
You hit it hard
And you plunge into its depths.
That's trauma.
Your trauma is dark and cold and confusing.
It tosses you around
And while you're in it, it feels like you have no direction.
You don't know which way is up and which is down.
You hold your breath even though your whole body is screaming
for air.
And then, without warning,
You break the surface.
But it doesn't end there.
You've barely started.
You struggle to stay afloat.
You struggle to find direction
While the waves keep crashing over you.
You fight to heal and it's not an easy fight by any means.
Those waves
Your brain
The thoughts that keep telling you to give in
Will fight you every time you try to swim.
And they don't fight fairly.
But the seas will calm,
It will get easier,
And one day you'll wake up and not know when it happened
But you'll know you grew.

You changed.
You healed a little bit.
That's not to say that the sea won't begin to rage again because it will.
But now you know how to swim.
The sea won't fight fair,
It will still throw everything it has at you.
But you have the upper hand this time.
You know what it's like now.
You're not going to fight fair either because you're done playing.
You'll roll with the waves until the storm passes.
In time
The storms will become more seldom
And smaller,
And some day you'll wake up on dry land,
Watching the beauty of the raging sea
Knowing that you survived it all.

TODAY, IN THERAPY

Life becomes so beautiful
When you're searching for beautiful things.

All of these little paper dreams,
Just strings
Of hopeful words it seems.
But I've always loved those sorts of things,
My little paper memories.

TODAY, IN THERAPY

I woke up today
And left my sense of dread in my bedroom.
I left my house
And kept my anxiety locked behind the door.
I drove to work with the windows down,
Letting my depression slip out the window like a stray grocery bag.
I had showered in positivity,
I had dressed in confidence.
Today, I will win.

Hey Mr. Daydreamer
What's going on behind your eyes?
Are your thoughts still in the stars?
Is your head still in the sky?
Hey Mr. Daydreamer
Is there still darkness in your mind?
Are you here with us this time,
Or did your fears make you go blind?
Hey Mr. Daydreamer
It's going to be okay.
Don't stress about your future.
Just make it through today.
Hey Mr. Daydreamer
Do you still feel alone at night?
Do you think about what could have been?
Do you still think it was right?
Hey Mr. Daydreamer
Those dreams are going to come true.
Stay the course, trust me,
I'm a daydreamer too.

TODAY, IN THERAPY

We're all living on borrowed time
And none of us really have a clue what we're supposed to be doing.
Live a little.
Relax.
Do your thing.
All the bull shit can wait for another sunrise.
It'll all be fine for another day,
I promise.

Do not bow to those whose respect only extends to the limit of your usefulness in their eyes.
Do not bow to those who act as if you are beneath them.
You are worthy of respect,
Especially your own.

TODAY, IN THERAPY

Dear older me
I'm sorry for fucking your life up.
And dear younger me
I forgive you.

Slow down.
Breathe.
It's going to be okay.
I promise.

22.
That number means something to me.
Does it mean anything to you?
22.
The number of servicemen and veterans
That the U.S. lets down every single day.
22.
The number who fought for us
Who we abandoned to the hell that became of their own minds.
Now,
I never served.
I couldn't even if I had wanted to
And even if I could have I probably wouldn't.
I don't do well with structure
But I digress.
Plenty of my family and friends did.
And I've known a few too many of those 22.
I've been fortunate
That everyone I knew made it back home.
But while they lived through the fight overseas it was the one that they fought
When they closed their eyes at night that killed them.
22 is too damn many.

The good days do come around.
Once in a while at least.
Keep your head up.
Carry on.

TODAY, IN THERAPY

"Strikes and gutters, ups and downs."
I think The Dude said it best.
Sometimes we just have to roll with the punches
And take the waves head on.
After all,
The Dude abides.

Go to therapy.
You don't have to tell anyone
Or spill out every emotion.
It takes real strength to ask for help
And I believe in you.
After all, you made it this far.
Go to therapy.

TODAY, IN THERAPY

When I set out to write this book, one of my main focuses was on men's mental health. Mental health in general is something that we still massively overlook as a society, especially when it comes to men. There is still a stigma around men's mental health and the challenges that we face. We are still expected to be providers and protectors and to always have the answers. We are expected to be the strong ones, and we are torn down when we can't be. When we need to ask for help, we are made to feel useless.

When I wrote this book, I wanted to make light of the issues that I myself have had and the issues that other men face every day. That's not to say that my only focus has been on men, but it was one aspect. I wanted to make light of the stigma and the double standards that we face in society each and every day. Society tells us to never be vulnerable, to never ask for help, to always put on a face. We are told to be the worker and provider instead of the artist and the creator. I wanted to break down some of those barriers and mentalities that have kept so many men unhappy for so long.

To the men reading this, please don't fall victim to the impression that you are meant to only be one thing. Please ask for help when you need it. Please don't be suffocated under the weight of always being the strong one. Find support in the people close to you and never be afraid to find professional help. One of the strongest things I have ever done was admitting that I had too many burdens to carry on my own.

I'd like to thank you for taking the time to read this. I'm hoping that you were able to find some meaning to these words. I'd also like to thank my friends who have been supportive of the process of finishing this book with all of their editing and review work. Also, thank you Brenda for the cover art.

Please follow my Instagram @ s.t.venema.writing and Facebook at S.T. Venema Writing. Don't forget to check out www.stvenemawriting.com for my blog and periodic updates on new projects.

Thanks!

-ST

TODAY, IN THERAPY

About the Author

Writer, Poet, Traveler, Dreamer

S.T. is a native Michigander and an avid outdoorsman. When he's not at home with his dogs he can usually be found hiking, biking, and kayaking any chance he gets. He is a vagabond at heart with a desire to experience the world and to share the world through his writing.

Currently, S.T. is in the process of his next book, so stay on the lookout for future projects.

www.ingramcontent.com/pod-product-compliance
Lightning Source LLC
Chambersburg PA
CBHW071952100426
42736CB00043B/3065